Sky*Boat

Sky*Boat
Poems and Collages

By Ronnie Burk

Edited by Mia Kirsi Stageberg

TRADE-MARK KOLOURMEIM OAKLAND, CA PRESS

ISBN 978-0-615-53558-6

Some of these poems first appeared in *The Barbed Wire Review, Big Bridge, The Café Review, Caliban, Cover, Exquisite Corpse (Cypercorpse), Ignite, Io, Jack Magazine, Magnus, Mesechabe, NY Arts Magazine, Orpheus Grid, UR*VOX* and *Verbal Abuse.* The quote by H.D. is from *Between History and Poetry: The Letters of H.D. and Norman Holmes Pearson,* Iowa City: University of Iowa Press, 1997, edited by Donna Krolick Hollenberg; as quoted in *Trilogy,* New York: New Directions, 1998.

To
Diane di Prima
Charles Henri Ford
Philip Lamantia

"I wish Aquarius would
get born before we
perish."
- H.D.

CONTENTS

EDITOR'S NOTE

The poetry of singular Latino surrealist Ronnie Burk was first published in *Caracol*, a literary magazine which I had the privilege to co-edit from 1974-1977. Over twenty-eight years of friendship, whenever Ronnie asked me for editorial advice he got it. If a line seemed obscure, I'd ask questions. If I thought he needed spelling or punctuation corrections, I offered them. Sometimes we went over a poem until he felt satisfied he'd worked it out. After all the back and forth of a long collegial friendship, I felt sanctioned to walk the road as his editor after his death, and am honored to have had the opportunity.

*Sky*Boat* was Ronnie's final manuscript, and I also looked at an earlier, spiral-bound version of the manuscript entitled *Inventory*, as well as versions published in his brightly colored chapbooks and on the Web. Over the years and in different drafts, he used differing systems of punctuation or line breaks, and I compared in order to standardize; whenever in doubt, I used my own recordings of Ronnie's readings to search for his voice and breath. I discarded a few poems that didn't seem his best, adding a few others I thought were strong and ought to be included. Five "original" ways in which his poems had been ordered became ten versions, as I worked to find Ronnie's right way. Eventually the work ordered itself, in a Ronnie-Burk-alchemical way.

Ronnie had an incredibly rich and interesting life, tough and hard-won. His challenges were the stark facts of his life, and he was often fueled as much by outrage at injustice as by a deeply passionate engagement with art and writing. His imagination tangled profoundly with surrealism, both visually and in words. Seeing his legacy taking shape, I find what he's left to us all the more precious for what it took in spirit and determination for him to bring it forth.

Special thanks to Elaine Katzenberger, Diane di Prima, Andrea Lindsay, and Garrett Caples, all believers in the force of Ronnie. Sit down and take it on if you can!

Mia Kirsi Stageberg
San Francisco, 2011

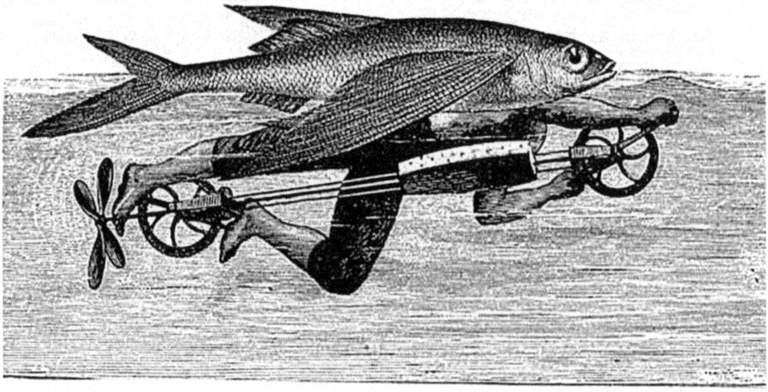

IN PRAISE OF SUN RA

SATURN RULES IN THE BLACK COLORS OF THE
RAINBOW SUN RA YOUR HAWK'S BEAK DEVOURING
THE SILENCE SUN RA WHAT IS THIS SOUND? IS IT
THE LOVE SONGS OF HOMOSEXUAL BLUE WHALES
FUCKING IN THE GREAT PACIFIC OCEAN? IS IT
FESTIVE TOADSTOOLS IN EMERALD-FEATHERED
MITRES OF THE PRIESTS OF TLALOC? IS IT A
FRACTAL IN THE PYTHAGOREAN EQUATION? SUN
RA THE TATTOOED MASKS OF POLYNESIA SWINGING
THE TEMPLE GONGS PAST FLOTATION BLARING
THE MANTRA OF EQUILIBRIUM (TIMBRE OF THE
EXPANDING UNIVERSE AS DEFINED BY THE WAVY
LINES OF OLD FATHER TIME) EXCORIATING THE
BLACK OOZE OF ORIGINAL MATTER CONDUCTING
A CHAOS OF ORDER INSTIGATING OUR MUTUAL
DEPARTURE ON THE GOLD WINGS OF A SCARAB
THEREBY UNDOING THE SAMSARIC SPELL CAST
UPON US FROM THE PLANET OF KARMA

MINERAL LIFE

The flaming wristwatches in her hair. Her teeth set with gold and azurite. Her white skin. How could I forget her standing beside an alabaster bust of Napoleon Bonaparte in a birdcage? Her powdered eyelids covered with butterfly wings that hypnotically fluttered at the thought of tar pits redolent of opalescent dew.

WEDNESDAYS

Glyph: green jewels tangible as a collection of *quetzal* plumes in a ball of *chicle.* Your calendar of days has high noon marked for a special get-together of intimate friends: Pancho Villa, Joseph Cornell, Billie Holiday. At the Teatro Chino the *rialtos* of future genius have just been toppled by another Californian earthquake. The stampede of emblems glittering in a white room full of pharaonic furniture. Everyone left orbiting the sun.

GENESIS

Blue girl swims through her day of dark suns. Mango blossoms on the pathway to the *cenote* of the central mountain. Devils in the rock cliffs consorting with monkeys to create a new race separate from all of us who had come from the sun. O my ancestors, ancient sky people, in blood fur and moccasins; can you make out the flat planes of this angular face? Beneath these curtains of raven hair the spirit guides are unavailable for photographing the red flowers with blood on that star.

SOL Y LUNA

sol

Blue sky what thoughts are you holding for me today?
Thousands of envelopes blow down the city streets
Each one crisp, clean, apparently brand new
My hand reaches down to pick one up
Inside is a tiny red heart
Can I create the feeling *this* is love?

luna

Feeding. Feeding the air blue moonlight. Feeding
the navel of the ocean wisdom. Feeding the earth
manure of human frailty.

Terra Firma. Before any earthquake: On a planet
full of craters we go digging for diamonds
in the black sands.

THE MARRIAGE OF HEAVEN & HELL

Chaos is my element when I go looking for Krishna Ma
        at Club Uranus
Infinities of the apparitional black hold, agog
A vial of sweet milk curdles in the mouth of a serpent
It is the Marriage of Heaven & Hell
Hysterical the radon-infested orgasm
That's Krishna Ma passing around the glass pipe
                tincture of dream life

TERRA INCOGNITA

to Tommy Turner

Above the black planet burning from sleep
no one recognizes you
but the black dot expands
where you think you are
caught in a mosaic of intersecting points
distilled from vapors of pure air liquido
perpetually circling the meridians
of the black star implosion

Deep inside the belly of the earth
a green gnome lives inside a silver chest
White spiders in the opal mines
Peeling back the edges of the world, you discover
termites, interstellar dust, plaster-of-paris

MIRROR OF WATER

The caterpillar that rests
on the twig
of his eyebrows
waiting for his certain
metamorphosis
The silver-threaded sateen finish
of his complexion
running down to his fiery core
The insignia of Saturn
on his forehead
illuminating a geography
of bituminous cities
held up by a tidal wave
in a mirror of water

BLUE PLANET (AFRICA)

A bony finger scratches the surface
of blue planet (Africa)
animating the burnt trees
riddled with hieroglyphs
A spiral staircase
on the back
of a snail
reaches for the mica-sliced window
framed in orange groves
that giant iris oblivious
to the stars' cascade

Tomato Girl in beaver shoes
cuts through the iron horse
trapped in the wall
the sun's bear claws
hung from the rafters
paved with root systems
the rat's own poison sprinkled
in the oven-colored eyes
of your moustache
erasing water

ADVENT OF THE REAL

On oceans of black milk
across airwaves of telepathic bliss
I have seen your other face
nimbus of nothing shining in the dark
pistil of your necromantic shadow
enigmatic to my sphinxian glow
You've made me delirious with your presence
honey of your belly smeared with coconut oil
your genitals taste of sea salt & pasta fruit salad
In a moment of utter despondency
I mistook you for Jesus Christ
levitating above the nonbelievers
ten thousand feet in the air
draped in cane smoke I declare you
fortress of the enormous orchid flower
wilting to rice paper

TOURISTS

Crablike the women wear jewels on
    their claws
Their men are red and wear straw hats
    to keep off the sun
Sea foam on their lips recalls the
opening of the crevices of the coral
waters

Salt licks at their bones

FAMINE CHARMING THE SNAKE OF ITS VENOM

SEAHORSES HAVE LEFT THE STRAW OF THE WIND
FORCED TO SWEEP THE STREETS OF LOBSTER CITY
DRUNKEN DOGS
SWIM IN LARD-INFESTED JELLY JARS *DE PURA MANTECA*
VAPORIZED BY THE ALCOHOLIC CONTENT OF A MARTINI
A *MUERTITO* IN PETTICOATS FLIES OUT THE WINDOW
CUAUTEMOC'S YELLOW ARSENIC POISONING
WEAVING A SPELL OF PROTECTION
HAVING KNOWN THE FIRST TRUTH, THE TRUTH OF SUFFERING
CAPTAIN COOK'S SYPHILITIC BANDAGES
DESIGNATE THE TOWER'S CALLOUS FEET
UNABLE TO CLIMB THE STEPS OF THE JIGSAW PUZZLE

CUAUHTEMOC

On embankments of flame born in the prophetic hour of broken windows, body paint unglued dresser drawers fly out from the marble side of your perfect torso. Mercury thermometers register degrees of the brain's own tumescent fish-fry at The Mudslide Café. Your mouth pinned with pheasant wings peppered with grave dust. Your fingers gone mad on the woodworking stone. Your cedar-packed limousines bludgeoned to anthracite corpses. Hung on meat hooks, the family tree is a ceiba stump bought and sold in the gringo stores of swamp savannah night.

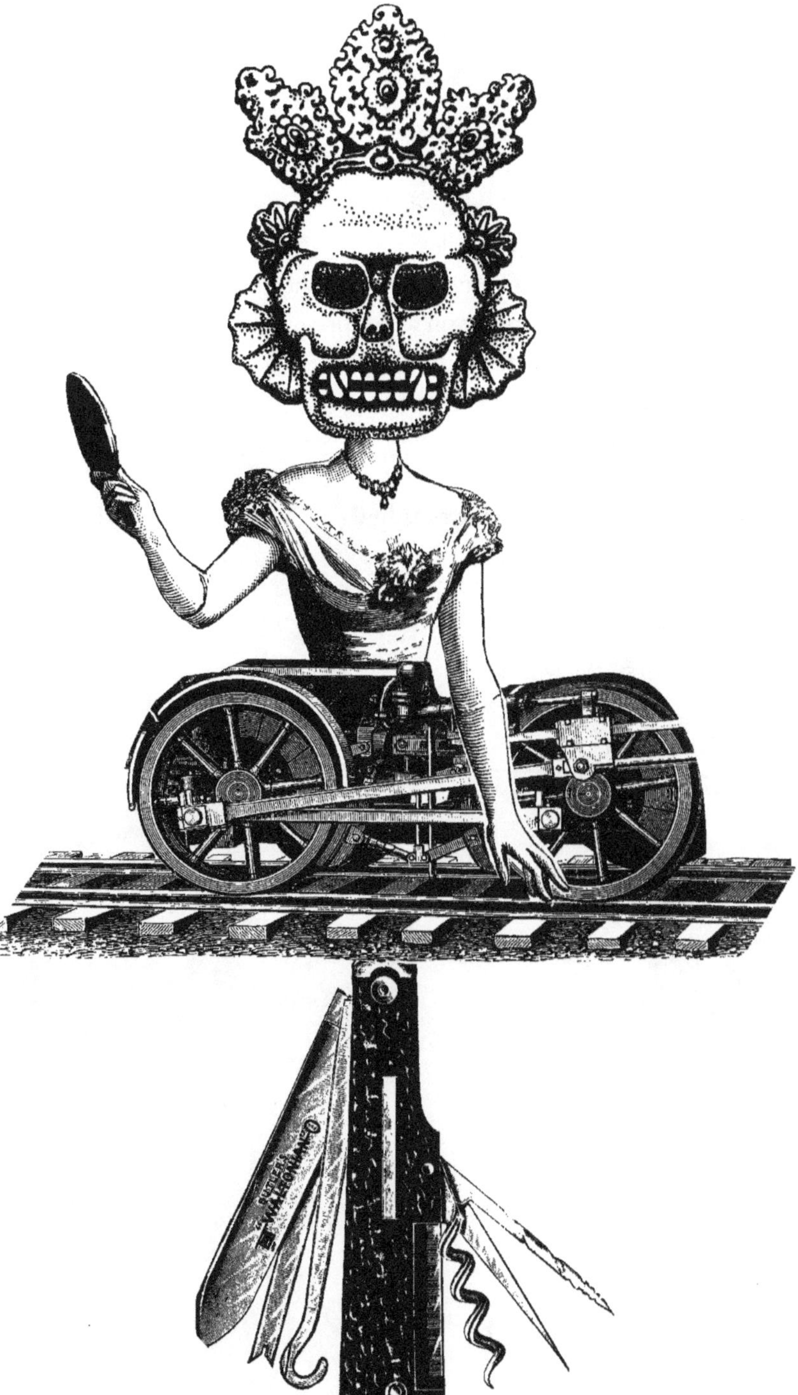

XIPE TOTEC

Xipe Totec soaking in Epsom salts
The centipede that lives inside him
Stitched with cactus needles
Slithers back into its protective nerve sheathing
His healing hand strung on a red thread
Tied around his chest of burning water
Sipping a cup of stinging nettles
To ease the pain

A dragonfly lands on the coastline
Of his missing finger
Having flown in straight from Hell
A lake of perfume ascends
The top of the world

Fangs of the sun
Undress me

POEM

The pyramid's hand directs the compass
Of the scorpion circle
The wheels of your eyes
Swollen to orange halves
Need I tell you
It's raining red lizard shit
Across the apex of day
The planes & angles
Of the industrial diamond
Lodged in your throat
Emit a charge
Attracting night moths
To the vagrant shadow
No one dare claim
The plumes of black snow
Melting to oil flame

FATHER OF REASON DAUGHTER OF DOUBT

Father of Reason, Daughter of Doubt
African bees are nesting
On the rooftops
Mercurio's phrenological head swimming
The skies of green foam
Polluting black tar honey
Lady Cyclops filled to the brim
    with milk opal
Stuffing her nightshirt full of
Ephedra's wooden mandibles
    concentric
The circles of her voluptuous rose
    mandala
Living at the edge of a world
Held up with chopsticks
Currents of air evaporate
Into buckets of boiling rain water

1996

The White Buffalo has left for the moon
The missing arms of Venus de Milo
Sweep up a shiny nickel
Amongst the marble trees
The seals of the earth covered in quicklime
The ancestral pit of bones broken
Open this grave we, somehow, live in

Chinese sparklers clear the way
Fountains from which I can see you
"Waltzing Matilda" of the hereafter
There's nothing to do

Vegetable curses
Vampire nurses
Madame Blavatsky puts on her shark fin corset
Televangelical
Apparition of Jesus & The Sewage Trust Fund
It's all a mirage

Green lions at their battle stations
Bes the dwarf embossed on a cornice of jade
Molten dragons the golden city born from a cupboard
full of *shabtis*
The Corn Maidens have left their sky compartments
White doe moccasins
doing somersaults on a high wire
salt serpent
rose is the diagram
I am looking for the crystal point
the world revolves on

That snake of feathers
rainbowed
in a hoop of dew

Mr. Fixit's typewritten a coded message
O'ahu's The Land of Adam Kadmon
Auntie Brake Lock on the beltway in Zodiac City
Metal detecting ice blue snow
In a coconut grove
A *gamelan* orchestra
On an intricately carved barge of teakwood
Sinks a hairline fracture into you my alabaster freezer
Window box gardening fluid star growth

Joseph lives! in the spherical dreams of a little girl's
soap commercial
King Kamehameha in Moctezuma's headdress
His face fading on a wet slab of obsidian
Dracula administering injections of frozen buddhas
Mirroring the sky's own discarded backbone
wet from rosewater
Frida's diary opens on Nosferatu's head
in The Crystal Cabinet of Dr. Caligari
Hawking snake oil at the Money Hole Brewery
Kamakura riding the light-switchback to Hell

•

photo
Photo-Mantic
I was born
bonsai-ed
in a Texas Tavern

fifty years
before The Great War
burnt holes
in the ceiling of
the World

•

Old Man Fishhead has a graybeard infested with termites
The Turtle People will have their revenge!
Spiderman up from the cement steps of Manhattan's
underground
His myth falls upon my Aztec profile
Climbing out from behind the astral curtains of
Crab-latitude-hemisphere
Hernan's a strange bird!
Wearing the helmet of a man-sawed-in-half
The zebra coiled pump fuse pillow
framing his Greco-Roman head
at an abandoned train station
circa 1910. His best friend
Moses Brushfire's aspirin tablet crumbling to red dust oblivion.
In his gold inlaid cartouche a set of crocodile tears
Saturn's clock on the table, cup & ball, child & saucer
in a marble tub taking a milk bath

•

Sirens in a glass bell float down rivers of
ayurvedic hair
The swan at battle for the diamond-spoked
color wheel
Flower labels a stick on body for Imenhotep

The Fool in the position of The Hanged Man
dissolving in acetone
The white owl lying face down is not my grandmother in a lei

•

The gargoyle at the bar just had a stiff drink
Wine soaked the scorpion fish baking
Your hind leg potato
That's why they call the Pope's nose
        a turkey butt
Shipwreck on a glass tower
The city draped in furs
Pig snout in a nun's habit
as only Hieronymus could paint it
Ambrosial palette of the hermetic rose pill
Scrying the abalone shell of water
Three crowns crash into a mirror
Forecasts The Black Hole Traveler
of Nineteen ninety-nine
The circle of demons bound by a red thread
Serving platters of toasted manta rays
Despite a belly full of birds-in-a-nest
Old Gringo's handcuffed
My Brother's Skeleton Key
Lono's hole of magma smoking rock

ENTOMBED

Unfurling a banner for
"A Butcher's Holiday"
a tin of laminated sardines
        arrives
Begging for more potash
Bela Lugosi's armpit scratches dead air
Powahatan smoking old fires in the streets

aquatic steroids

All these corrosions beneath the shell of
my reckless heart
my heart of sliced throats
my heart of Aztec tendons
my syphilitic heart of lily-headed serpents
ready to attack the creators of
The Poison Milk Factory

demon in a dressing gown
the sugar seals
a satin slipper
sputtering the fragrance
Piss Angel

It is at this point we step into the cyclone
to embrace here and there
Moments of the sixth dawn
Crocodile banks of the Nile float on Tenochtitlán Highway
as polluted cities sink beneath the horizon of crazed Empire
Ancient castles wash up on the foreheads of black-rock
        mountains

Pulling the tip of your beard with the hand of a leprechaun
Your deerhunter's cap brings a scene from a movie
& I am reminded it is The Saturn Return of The Chicano
    Movement
Having cracked the egg of hard-boiled reason
        fever
        light
People gather in the courtyard to watch the cobra
marry the hawk on my head
Fat baby Caduceus, I'm through!

POEM: NEW MEXICO
JANUARY 3rd, 1997

Pele's the raven throne up above the thunderous *metate* stones
Arctic claws a continent of ice
The deer children are dancing on high rock mesa
To spear the heart of the sun
Butterfly Maidens hold rainbows over slopes of cascading snow
Down below, white flowers bloom in the *arroyo*
There is the smell of Tibet on the mountain
Golden junipers walk with me on the road to Acoma
Otter boy swims in the icy streams just beneath the ravine
Pine spirits hoot owl light

YVES TANGUY

The green veins of his hands of cigarette smoke
Fold over the spidernails of Herman's coffin.
Sunk in a vat of flesh-eating maggots,
Soils of my heart
Cast an oblong shadow across the wall
Turmoil of a petroleum sunset
Spinning elastic threads to tie the trees up
With smog-control devices
Birds less repulsive than pigeons
Make love in the dark.
Salvaging pitchforks of rotten hay
Dead Indians survive the plate-glass world

OPENING THE GRAVEYARD DOOR TO THE HUMAN-FACED HYDRA

A BLACK SPIDER CRAWLS INTO THE ZODIAC
HUMMING TOMORROW'S VIBRATION
HATSHEPSUT'S VULTURE-BEAKED MUTATION
CRASHING THE UPSIDE-DOWN LOCOMOTIVE'S
RADIUM CURE
DISSOLVING TUMORS TO RAVEN FEATHERS
COBRA SKINS FLAY THE LIGHT SPARKING
THE HEXAGRAM OF DESTRUCTION

MOTHER OF MONSTERS

The doctor opened your mouth
To show me the bacilli
That live inside you
The nurse scraped your vagina
For the mortar they use
In the tombs of vampires
Mother of Monsters
I am your child

THE OLD MAN OF THE MOUNTAIN

The Old Man of the Mountain comes down from his cave. He says: to conjure Mother Nature in a mirror, place a pair of antlers in a pool of stag's blood. Maggots contaminated with pesticides eat at the corpses in the terrarium of the world. Covered in shrink-wrap a gas explosion falls asleep in a rainbow of crystal vapors. His left leg forms from a blossoming apple tree to crawl up through the hole of Asia. A black toad descends into the fire pit of the asbestos dragon. This is the first tincture: sugar of lead.

TO WED FIRE

To wed fire to air: the mercurial sperm must be tossed into the vessel with a pinch of arsenic. A pile of gold dust to tip The Scales of Libra. You've now passed from nigredo to the point of dismemberment. Droplets of black rain on the back of a swan push down skeletons of rotting milkweed. Microwaved. Ravens pick at your remains. A scroll of sheet music to tone the spheres. In the last chapter lions devour each other in Her Majesty's very own audio-hallucinatory fugue. Aleph, that pillar of cloud hovering over The Walls of The Cast-Iron City, told the story of two fat cupids in a glass jar.

BLACK TULIP

Mating in Elysian Fields horned lions are tearing at each other. The meat of angels sliced to little orange poison pills. Your head blossoming the steel conjunction of Mars. Heavenly centaur, your job is to draw the star from the flower. In Siberia Iron Planet Jesus walks on water. Instamatic Jesus of the last two thousand years burnt to a crisp. Beneath the boiling waters lobsters scream for their terrified lives. A crayfish draws a diagram of a dissected human. All the organs labeled with a number and a planet. In a glass furnace dolls are melting—hair, teeth and eyes. Yahweh's mind evaporating a thin-out coating of high octane [viral loads] the image of Shiva on a couch of tiger skins. The Orishas in the celestial vault working overtime.

PRIAPUS

Deep within the catacombs of myself I have gathered bent nails of torn-down houses, fragrant skeins of perfumed silk, broken dolls of confused pretension, auguries foretelling the doom of mankind, soft orange glowing pesticides. Even if the salt packs dredged up a mummy factory I'd still be in the swing of things.

TEMPTRESS MOON

In the ancestral hall
I burn
termite-infested
statues of rotting saints,
the names of dead gods,
& bent syringes

MY LIFE, MY ABANDONED HOUSE

I'm afraid I'll discover
radiation burns on the wall
since my iguana-headed lover left me
lead flakes peeling the skin
back
this blistered apartment
has taken on an oven
glow

An avalanche of asphalt
has crushed the stairway
the windows have all grown fangs
rusty asteroid in the toilet bowl
ceiling crashing to surround you
            mercury
            doorway

SACRED HEART

To bend back the black sheets of
aluminum foil & fold the
black metal rose of asphyxiation

There are no more cannibals to lunch on
the cogs & wheels of last night's
torture machines
Only this sheet of metal to bend back
the image of your televised face
flickering in the windows of
your meat heart

yet to be eaten

HIGH FREQUENCY

Geryon's the first monster to leave the room
The planets move on high wires
The clock of the world is held together
with masking tape
Bug spray, hair spray, deodorants, fluorocarbons,
roach pills, neurotoxic shampoos & rug cleaner
were only a few of the items I saw in her medicine chest
Heart of the spider weaving this spell
A tiny incision in the fur coat of Grandmother Spider
knitting the constellations
Having given back the lingerie of the Holy Virgin
Polluted air forced me to grow gills

•

You cannot kill *amaku'a* without incurring a karma
impossible to rectify
Now that all the porpoises have committed suicide
nostalgic for life before the whiteman arrived
I had a bowl of *poi,* sat down on tin can beach
& ate a banana
fragrant banana flower dripping with flower sperm
You cannot kill *amaku'a* without bombing your children's
children to genetic malevolence
So much for your fetal obsession meeting its wax double!
Take a vacation to neon cities return to TV
Eat plastic food & vomit your bile-soaked brain
with assorted chemotherapeutic poisons
Bury lead tooth-marks of uranium bullets
in all the breasts of Diana
Whatever you do just remember

you cannot kill *amaku'a* without putting a scowl
on the face of Nuestra Señora de los Remedios

•

Wolf boy sharpens his claws pressing wormwood
through a meat grinder
Giant spider in a maze working the lattice
of the radium screw

Thunder is loose in Hercules' mineral bath
Dipped in starlight the planets
whirl on out to metamorphose
new halos of the human larvae

Chrysalis in a purple ray

Banded with the seven colors
black flowers droop
in a dissolving shower of methadone

Stalagmite the crystal magnet of the horse ghost nostril

NIGHTMARE

Dust
the presence of you
in all your hunchback
silence
you sleep with
anger
knives
thunder
scorpions

There is no remedy for the serpent
writhing
in our bellies
belching
alcohol
flowers
I'm listening for the lice nesting
in your armpits & the sudden
crackling silence of a shriek
torn from the mouth of a corpse
I once knew

DREAM

His wolf cheeks
in a box of
ragweed
Torn-up
cobblestones
litter
the alleyway,
a vial of mercury
suffuses his silver skin
Or is it moonlight coursing through his
transparent veins?

Horse
coach
buggy
a fragrance of perfumed death
in his dressing room
I mistake for a vampire
His bat child
His monster child
His ice child strangled in a polished mirror

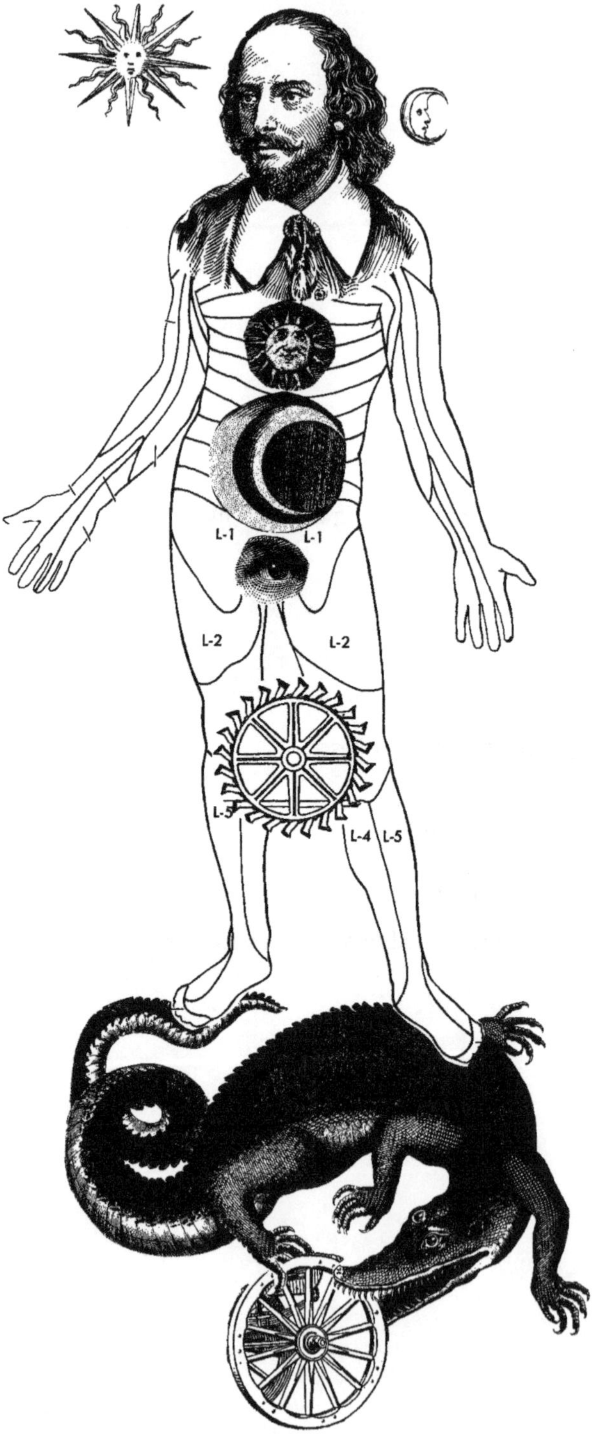

L-1
L-1
L-2
L-2
L-5
L-4
L-5

TELEGRAM

THE HAIRBRAINED BIRD RESTS ITS FEATHER-BRUSH SKELETON ON THE AERIAL MAPS OF ALLUVIAL DEW. EVEN IF THE POOL CUE FOUGHT THE CRAB THE ROUTE TO THE WATERCRESS CHAMBER WOULD BE ABOUT THE SAME DISTANCE AS THE INTESTINES OF A TRANSPARENT BIRD.

THE GULLIES WORRY ABOUT THE RIVERS, THE RIVERS WORRY ABOUT THE FORESTS, THE FORESTS WORRY ABOUT THE MOUNTAINS. BUT THE LAKES! THOSE TURQUOISE LAKES OF GREEN SNOW HAD BETTER FORGET ABOUT EVER JOINING THE HATPIN MOUSTACHE FOR LUNCH.

COCKATOO BIRD SNAKE. QUETZALCOATL. BONE DRILL.

THE SCALPEL LEFT THE SWITCHBLADE BEHIND TO DISSECT THE RED BIRD ORGAN WHILE THE DRAINPIPE RAN OFF THE WATER TABLE TO SHORT-CIRCUIT THE PLANKTON-FISH-SPINE ELECTRODE UNIT.

THE CONSTELLATIONS

These, then, are the constellations that swim within the currents of his flesh. There is the scorpion's milky flower. There is Draco's swirling nebula. There is the burnt star of all his nerve endings. There is the fishtail of his gold leaf terrace.

OBSESSIVE LOVE

To live in terror of it
Its strange blossom
already wilted
before it gets
started
The claw of all its
beginnings

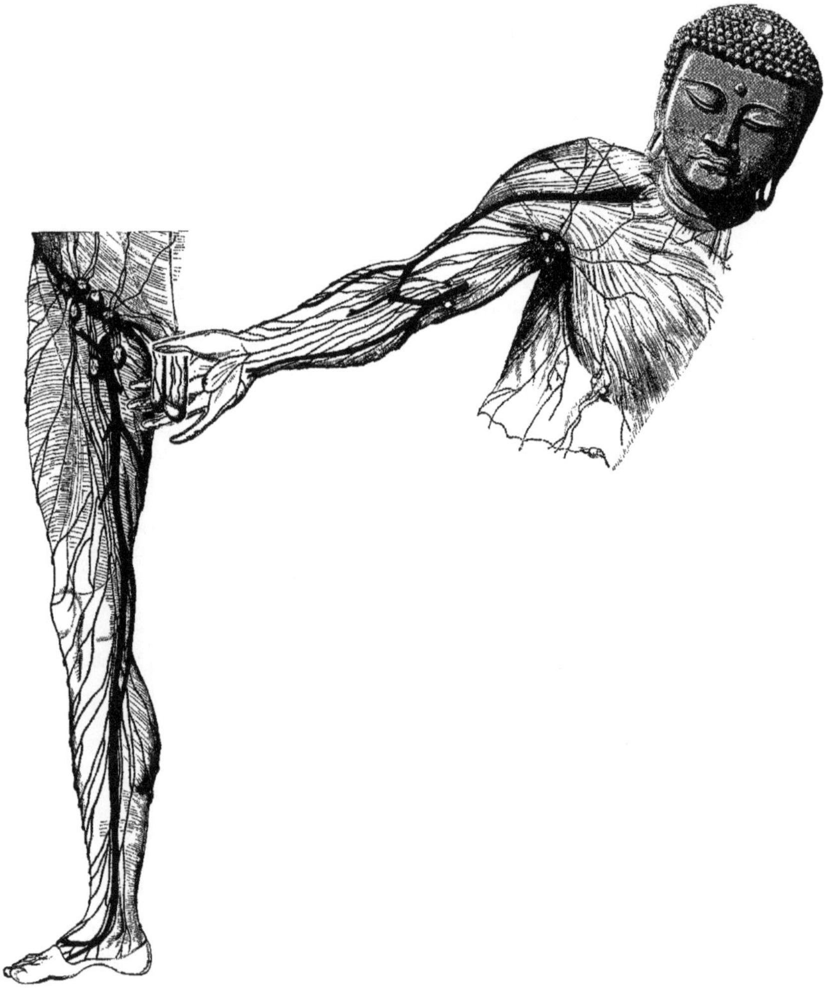

CAÑA

Sad-eyed lover
I mend your broken parts
& chew you like a piece of
sugar cane
to draw the sweetness from
within

YOUR HAIR

Filigree of sensation
sludge of pain
dirty rivers of contagion
floating corpses of the Ganga
sewers of sex
My heart sleeps there
covered with lunation cycles
oblivious,
slightly disturbed,
a little paranoid,
a frightened animal held together
with leopard skins & scarabs
My heart sleeps in a velvet current
aching, restless, wanting
only you

MAGIC SPELL

He is father of Old Father Time
even though he is himself
a child
He is wicked laughter down a drunken alleyway
& I am both serpent & star twisting endlessly
round his perfect body

INVENTORY

four eyes
four arms
four legs
two heads

MEDUSA

I have shrunk to a twig watching
your beautiful face covered with ivy & sunlight
What can I say?
I have fallen into the hole of your galaxy
wanting passage into the entranceway of your heart
I snuck past the guard at checkpoint
opening a valise I gave you
razors,
toothpaste,
shaving cream
Red jade grasshoppers came to haunt my garden
Yes! I even tried to humor you with love
Seeing my body as an opportunity for joy
I ran into the surf holding your severed head above the sea
the pleasure was all mine

WORDS WRITTEN IN BLUE FLAME

Horus-the-strong-bull-loving-truth
etches the world in place
snake-born kabala in an abandoned
factory yard
ominous as an upside-down 3
little girls fly down the hotel hallway
glowing mirrors of the kidnapped Infanta

steel blade
Electra
lacerating
newsprint
people

domino theories confront the irrational factor
bloody crustacean stuck between the crevices devouring Man

stopwatch
pelvis
vibrating discs of
pure pleasure
sex burns taboos of the gods
a hint of Africa in the bluer waters
weaving
peyote eyes,
emerald daggers,
quetzal plumes,
thunderbolt
dorjes,
footbinding the skyscraper

in silk pajamas
even the Olmec mask can't hide
your lies

CARTE BLANCHE

NEW YORK HAS A WAY OF PICKING THE LICE OUT
    OF
THE HAIR OF A FAULTLESS WOMAN
SHUCKING THE CORNHUSKS OF CATHEDRAL
    WINDOWS
A FALCON HIDES BETWEEN THE PAGES
HAVING BENT THE ACROBAT BACK INTO A BOX
INSIDE A PHONE BOOTH
AUNT MATILDA INSTRUCTS LITTLE AMY
ON THE SKILLS OF RUBY CUTTING
SNAKING HIS WAY TO LEFT FIELD
A WEREWOLF PICKS HIS TEETH
LOOSING A PYTHON ONTO A STEAMSHIP TO
    ICELAND
HUMAN MEAT CAN BE QUITE APPETIZING

HOTEL ZIGGURAT

He is buried around here
somewhere
in these caves of gold-on-black ore
Gladiators go to battle
within an immense emerald
spinning
metal threads over
the head of a Roman emperor

Saturn runs down each descending
ladder
rung, level, scale to Hell
Globes of liquid gold
in a centrifuge
might be worlds
in a crystal cabinet
William Blake in there
spinning a nourishing, life-sustaining
terrestrial web

There is no elevator
escalator
We take the stairwell
ladder
scaffold
to the next rung

The world is a high-rise
hotel
ziggurat
skyscraper

Hinged at the edge of a rippling ocean
cosmos
universe

forever under construction
the roof is on fire

DEEP IN THE BOWELS OF THE CAST-IRON CITY

High atop Cleopatra's flying needle galaxies are birthing tangled webs of lightning emptying rivers of *plata* into the diamond-engraved incunabulum of divine formulae.

Hans Bellmer on the cobblestone walkway to the maimed doll's house. The inner glow of his jaguar eyes pierced with the light of solar regions. Corrugated the wire that holds him together. In his hand a pendulum swings tiny vortices that give way to phases of eclipse. The miracle is in how a guitar floats through the parlor of his pearl-smitten hair as he looks for you hiding behind skyscrapers wrapped in tin foil.

Rearranging the angular black mantle stones inscribed with white powder the scorpion-faced lady in the linoleum wig fends off a school of iron-gloved piranhas attempting to attack her half-eaten octopus. Outside the abandoned tenement a black dog chases its tail and bursts into flames, as a butchered horse clodhopping the plaza littered with flayed spider lilies forages for food in drippings of dogwood tallow.

My saber-tooth lobster eating Detroit eating Manhattan eating the airplanes dumping clouds of red dust on the conflagration down below.

BASILISK

The sun is bleeding
Bloodshot eyes
of tortured animals
Flaming stones of
torn entrails
Boiling crows
possess me

ROTTING MANSIONS

Resuscitating Fedrico's lover crash zone oracle gas tanks
suicidal thoughts of cigar store Indians burning in a cornfield.

Bolting, not strapping, experiencing uncontrollable laughter,
bricklayers forfeit easily assembled coffin chairs to slaughter
chimeras in an arcade.

DEAD ENGINES

Beneath the wheels of a locomotive, severed fingers,
broken bones ground to sugar dust, asphalt
stones, hills of beer cans & mountains of
decomposing bodies
Beneath the wheels of a locomotive, three-eyed demons whirl
menacing tornados of destructive forces,
world wars, burning cities, rust of junk cars &
shards of piled-up sheet metal spinning tombs of
mass death
O my ancestors! Caught beneath the wheels of a locomotive
uranium babies burn
napalm hauled to the breeding grounds of
buffaloes stampeding dust storms of
idle machinery

MEXICAN PROVERB

A cop, a rug and a piñata are best when beaten.

SURREALIST PROVERB

Sweep the laundry, fold the floor, cook the window, bake the door.

ZEN HAIKU

although/ we sit in the pond/
the piranhas/ have not/
bothered us/

TITLES

My Lover Owns An Emerald
Flesh Garden
Conquistador
Mapping The Star Holocaust
There Is A World Under The Table
Princess Of The Cranes
The Gods Are Standing By

IN MY ROOM

The face of twigs on the bedroom
wall
blinks & fades away in the afternoon
sunlight
My solemn head
anointed with fever
mechanically
teeters & totters & finally falls off
its pedestal

A MAN

A man's face is long
& weary
bound with wire
& held together with sheet rock
plaster

A man's tears are bitter
opium
A prayer to a dead god
A foolish vice

A man lives in my brain
sullen & hapless
A frozen image of deadly poison
waiting to thaw

TURQUOISE ROCK

She is standing above the clouds of
Lake Chapala
The lake is famous for scrying
the towns & castles built on the back of
a griffin

My mother was a demoness
she tells me
I still placate her with polished carnelians,
antique brooches
fragile finery
too delicate for a man's touch

Lost in a candelabra
she returns to the labyrinthine
drawers of her sepulcher
mah-jong box
Drawing the curtains back
she finds herself
crumpled face in a core of magma

CRYSTAL

On crystal you can really see
the paranoid visions of America
Pilgrims in their automobiles
maneuvering the endless
clutches and stick shifts
to mutually measured destruction.
For safety measures
I require poetic license
with nuclear dust.
Phantom Indians in cemeteries
remove the cruel hearts
of certain whitemen.
They say,
Don't forget Sitting Bull
Crazy Horse, Geronimo
Your grandfather Cuauhtemoc
too!

MAN-OF-WAR

to Lynn Randolph

With a stab to the head of technocracy
a marsupial in flight goggles
takes us to a place where
gardenia,
fish
& woman
are all one
star

Torture rooms of ecstasy,
laser wars of future conflagration,
baboon in a blown-up refinery,
riding a satellite
to the hidden highway ghettos of the mind,
bored with syringes and test-tube babies,
little men on a chessboard
go to battle
as
mankind's cloning machine switches on
war

1999

to Mumia Abu-Jamal

slaveship America your mutiny held back with a radium pin. Electrocution short-circuits the amphibious arms merchant.

up from the subterranean caverns of prehistoric water

The History of America is written in pig's blood. Human hair entangles the story. George Washington salutes the dollar sinking into the shit holes of time. Meltdown of the chrome-plated people. Lead-encased pellets, uranium bullets, the steamy earth rumbles volcanic stones thrown into the face of Pele's fury.

cracked visage of light

America your torn-down houses have festered long enough! Fog takes the shapes of my ancestors massacred in the purple night flowers—henbane, belladonna, and mandrake. If nectar is nightshade I curse you with mandrake spears daubed in the earwax of Betsy Ross' vaginal membrane.

666 emblazons a bust of Helen. Her veiled appearances on all your warships heading for conquest makes clear your Empire is destined for burnt-out Plutonic nightmare.

MY DEATH

My death has a baboon's head
alligator teeth
eat the flames
of his evil spells
pierced lovers embrace
wheels of naked bodies
vedic pills
burning tigers of your solar mansions
transparent splendors
narcotic paradise
lingam & missile
on a desolate landscape of fixed bauxite
My death sits shimmering
a black hole of reconnaissance
tied up with white
altar scarves
smoking mule-faced
cigars

IRON LIONS

Lost kings of Atlantis
it's always the same old story
written across a pharaoh's beard
fate of Saturn
rattling
steel bars
on Mission St. the arrows point neon
doom lipstick torture
Circe your brassiere strap hung on
the moon
Circe your crown of cow horns unravels the mystery
of Sirius
your name uttered in blue light
Circe I hear the words spoken in broken English
lion's wing, compact mirror, drifting midget
at a bus stop
I recognize you from a 16th century
engraving
on the way to the Inquisitor's chamber
& I am mad for the extraterrestrial
walk-in children
who sleep in the doorways of abandoned buildings

UNCONSCIOUS MOTIVE

Viewed from the blinking eye of a cormorant
zeppelins target the Pope's miter
Faster than buses & bicycles
the motors & engines
folding the air
while the glue catches
the amount of time borrowed, time stolen,
time clocked in
looking for lunar moths,
poltergeists,
carpet-burning
chandeliers,
touched by cross-wires
forgiving no confusion
Who will arrest my face
covered with lobster tails?

INCANTATION

for the homeless

My house is made of raw silk,
fishweed & pickled daikon.
My house with the pearl
in the ointment. Abandoned
unsightly house at the end
of the road. My house of the
ten-thousand rooftops of Shanghai.
Hotel room. Train station. Jet terminal.
My house of broken wheels.
My house with the witch cap.
Burning house of paper screens &
sliding doors. My house of adobe
in the turquoise sunlight.

SKY*BOAT
to Will Alexander

In the Horned Kingdom Cernunnos traces the veins
 of Jerusalem
To a cracked cistern in a field of poppy flowers
My kabalistic egg hatching the Sephiroth of the Lost
 Planetary System
Iron plumes of the ten thousand eyes of Ezekiel's Beast
Swirling a cyclone of black coronas
His *vajra* of coffin nails and colored threads
Tied with burnt cherub medallions

In the apparition zone having set fire to water
Rabid dogs dance in a fusion of tungsten light
Inflorescence of that Little Man in the bottle
Separating the salt from the ash
The Tormented Mermaid searches for her children
Abandoned in the sewers of the world
Density of carbon auroras fishing for a pearl
In the tributaries of a majestic keyhole
Manta rays return to the lake of blood

My mother in her lunar costume beating Hydra's wing

•

Uruborus of my third eye curled up in a mollusk
Hekate's gallery sails over the storm
Extracting rays from a nugget in a lead box
She knows nothing about the somnolent
Footsteps of the Philosopher's Widow
At the doorway to the dungeons of chaos

Pericles on a razor blade incubating quicksilver
Distilling filigree of disintegrating planet
Extinguishing Mars

•

When the peacock in the blue bottle attacks its mate
The crippled farmer knows it's time to water his silver trees
Holding a lantern of fireflies
A washerwoman pierces the diamondback salamander
Smoldering beneath the rocks
The royal couple poured into a gelatin cube
In the radium mines a necklace of thorns
Strangles the cross-eyed Gemini
Always the sun & moon in one face

•

In a moment Toussaint l'Ouverture will enter the turquoise
    morning of Nezahualcoyotl's calligraphy room
And place a lei upon Queen Lili'uokalani
Marking the *ve've'* of the Ruby Queen
On his left shoulder covered with epaulets
He will proclaim the sovereign rights for
The Constitution of The Garden of Earthly Delights
Heraldic star of Neptune's ray black jade insignia of the
    eagle-serpent
    on a column of *nopal* smoke
Demon-slayer of purified ore His child in the red suit is Chango
Guiding Erzulie's spangled boat in, to the face of Tlaloc
    in Aquarius
Ogun! Of the red squares chasing tigers in a black mirror
Always Taurus! Your mangled star in the chalkyard

Boiling the leper's cloth nursing the Century back to sleep
To keep disease from overriding the emaciated devi of the dried-up rice paddy
Uranium swallows the rats scurrying about the graves of suicide kings

COILED ROOM

Serapis wraps his snake tail around my own
his lingam my throne covered with sandalwood paste
Green waves beat against black rocks
frothing like milk churning another cosmos

Ornate fixtures of thunder and brass
Megaliths humming messages from above the world
Nuit weaves her night spell
The roof clear as a sheet of glass

Floating around the room as if you were underwater
Green fangs protrude from your blue skin
Your gills secreting silvery corpuscles
billions of them
glowing on the aether like fireflies

Radium blue
The temperature of light
Radium blue
The density of jewels
Radium blue
radiant against the cloudbanks,
slashed across lush savannahs,
verdant deltas,
vines of kudzu choking miles of forests,
glittering chunks of broken lapis thrown up against the sky

Exposing the sea grasses of your naked body
you open the eye of my heart
Weaving menacing black reptiles
you walk the calm earth

Pierced with arrows of tortured coyotes
you sleep underground
oblivious to all of this

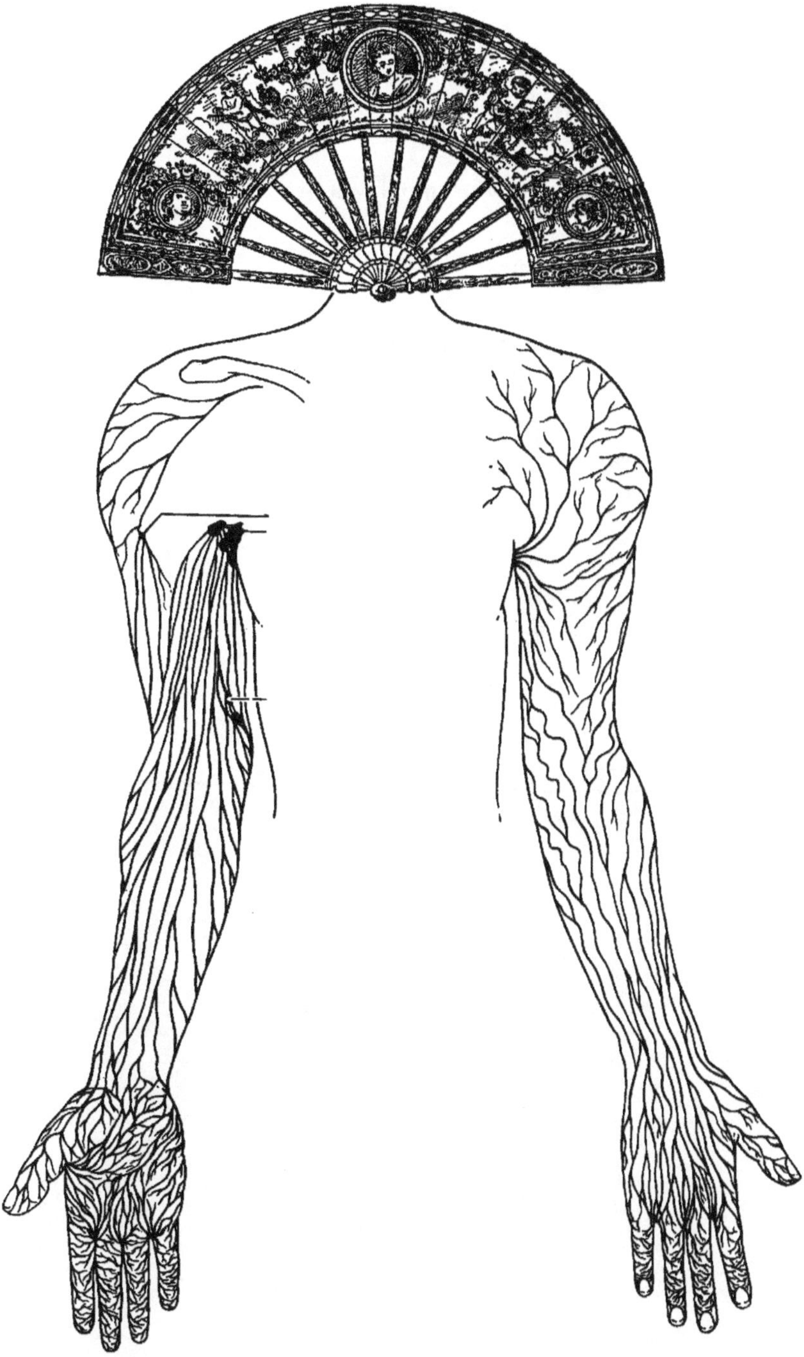

L'ARCHIBRAS

L'archibras floats along the limpid waters
looting crayfish
soaking heads in brine

Always sure to be carrying a fresh corpse with the old
the eye of Kali's scimitar
marries the bloodstained trident
boiling *morcillo*

OBSCURE MOMENT

Scrutiny of eyes
tortured looks
obscure formations
Everywhere I look I see you
transposed
pixilated
dissolved
rearranged into branches of flesh & stone
Only to find my mind erased
staring at nothing

SELF PORTRAIT, 2001

Scratched walls of asylums
drunken rhinos in churchyards
dustbins of flesh
lunatics of enraged ink
hanging pictures of zombies at deadbeat hotels
fissures of cracked china
stenciled horror of gas chambers
outmoded paranoia of faceless Buddhas
blown up to archaic smiles

FEVER

To suck the diamond
spinning
behind the tongue
of a corpse
a flower sweats
dying from its own
grief

twelve pills
the sleeping
machine's
chrome to touch
this side of you

hangnail is the serpent
raped of wisdom &
the lotus of sleep
returns the damage

OVAL FRAME

Somewhere between Vanderbilt and Flatbush Avenue
Sitting Bull & Marcus Garvey meet for the first time
smoking visions of the Montauk Club
Staghorns hang from an oval frame of J. P. Morgan
opening tombs for the tombless
eagles ascend the throne
Hovering over glass gardens of *fiesta del sol*
Oshun appears
crescent on a silver vessel riding the mercurial waters
gilded statuettes of the old gods of Egyps in the windows of
Mother Mary's Thrift Shop
Handing over my secret name to the starving ghosts of mass
    hallucination
heaven has a tin pressed ceiling

AMERICA

She is expensive but has cheap tastes
When she is not hallucinating clean water in a plastic bottle
she is spending money on facelifts
Bust implants and cancer-producing vaginal inserts
keep her happy

Choking in radium pills
Craving diet cokes & fat-free potato chips
Her fingers severing hands to do her shit work

Dipped in the flesh of dead Indians cooked in Texas chili sauce
Florida becomes a small penis stuck between her sagging breasts
The Andes form the topographies of her cellulite thighs
What is Mexico? if not the armpit of her muff
Masturbating to the droning sound of atomic explosions
Her plush existence held together with collateral damage

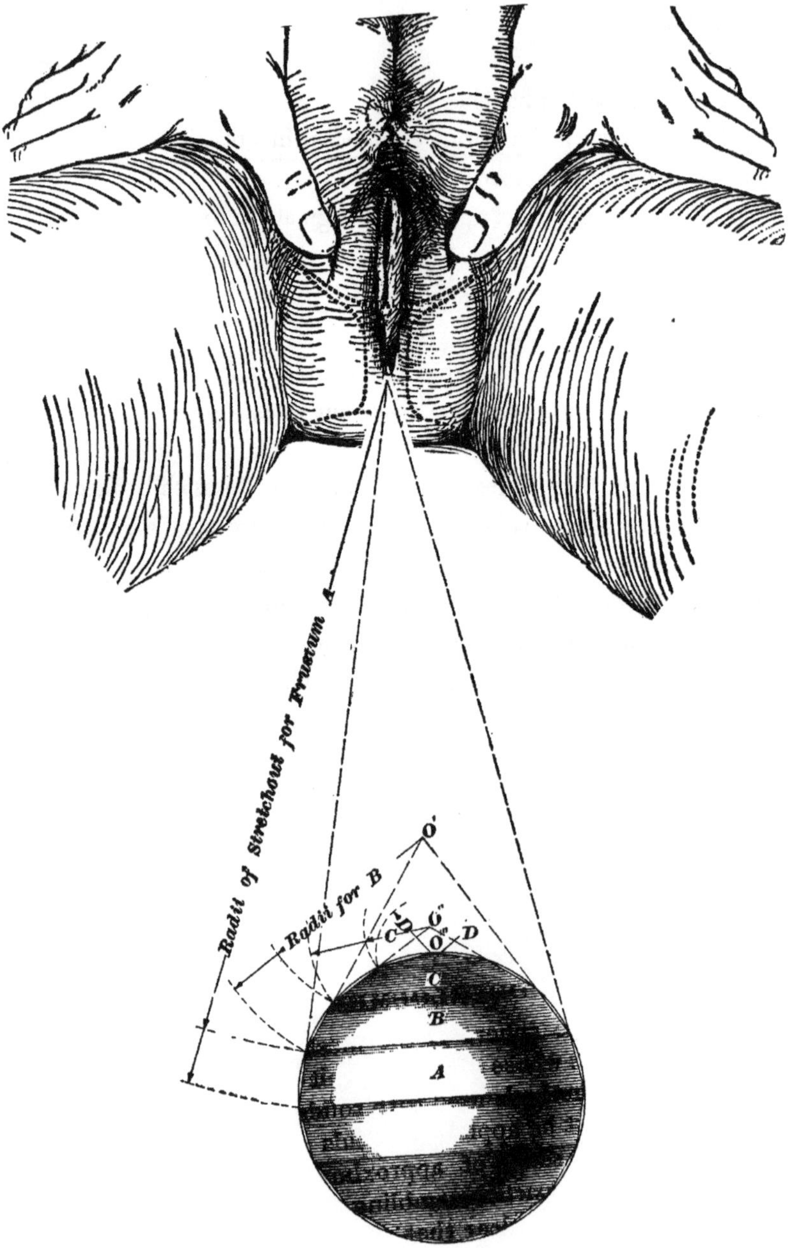
Radii of Stretchout for Frustum A
Radii for B
O'
C
D
O''
O
D
C
B
A

OSHUN

star above
the moon
moon above
the flower
flower above
the earth
earth above
the sea

RED LION

forcing open the mouths of certain flowers
tiny dragons of torn light pierce
amber crystals melting to glowing filaments
gold nuggets studded with ice green jewels
swim in the murky pond
shimmering depths of the curative waters
splintering seed in an iron box
your cup of snakes eats your raven
night & day swallowed whole
even if you placed every king on the Tree
the illuminated child would still preside
over a thicket of heart-shaped rosebuds
blooming in a bowl of air flagellating lovers
restore you to the solarized power of a red lion

THIRD EYE RAILROAD

Lone cloud above the chimney swept by angels
A million people ride the back of a tortoise
to a parade of mermaids
A midget stands on a rooftop
tearing a clock apart
as a decrepit building buckles from
Shiva's laughter

Kundalini jump rope
Climbing a ladder to nowhere
Claudius takes the L
Miserable Hierophant!
His book swings shut on its hinges
Grimacing urchin-faced creature,
secrete your ink, dictate your laws and be gone!
I swear by the clipped toenails of Nebuchadnezzar
baboons open The Gates To Hell

Invisible Leviathan, I see you like a tarot card
The Pope flapping his bat wing
to ward off the wrath of the backward-moving serpent
Flame-headed cherubs swirl light-waves of crumpled cellophane
melting faces of frightened women trapped in orbs

Orchestra of beetle-shaped men on the platform
what *is* life if not this Cubicularum of Nightmare / Dream
locked inside the coffin of a shrew mouse?
Lost On A Street of Marvels vigilant as a wooden hawk
I watch as a maze of people walk through turnstiles, walk
    through water,
walk through glass

ORNATE TIGERS

A hand reaches out of the incinerator twisting wires of holocaust
the stench of carnage in the shattered pavement of exploding
windows clouds of asbestos in the iron rain defecating ash strewn
saddhus the roar of Durga above the din of neon clashing metals
of burning gypsum crumbling to atomized cement cracking
fissures in the rock wounds boiling the paving stones to Hell.

TOWER CARD

Fountain of a thousand heads

Splintering the Siamese lion in half
your god is a toad swirling down a river of drowning horses

Majestic hour of rotting saints

Suffocating from a liniment of camphor and boiled feet
gates are crumbling to metal fumes poisonous with cancer

Moment of absolute destruction

Iron corset wrapped in flesh,
mechanical damsel
daughter of Coatlicue

Now it is your turn to watch the rats flee the Three Towers on
the hill

ALL SAINTS TAVERN

Scylla and her monster ride the zodiac
The Devil stands hunchback
to her gremlin in the bracken
Rotting witches stuck in the chimney
gift-wrap the buildings
House-hunting a clock full of angel hair,
congregations of duck-billed people
torment the dirty bride
Pouring kerosene on a dead branch
wild man Valentine burns his shoes
Hot key in a boiling cauldron
Ice diamond Isis of the Seas
caroling Crown Manor
You enter through the red chalk doorway
the hotel like living inside a cameo
Horned denizens of the pit sound the alarm
as a band of scaly women topple
Our Lord Jesus from his wooden cart

Hidden among checkerboard boxes
a giant's face floats down Ragpicker's Alley
Entrails of fishtails, mouths full of ash,
nailing their coffins shut
human crayfish go to their hole

UNICA ZÜRN

Guarding the coiled archway Elizabeth-of-the-quails
turns her prow towards the pole star
Entering the battle of the eagle-headed hydras
a necklace of human heads
encircles the embroidery of her *grimoire*

Odyssey of shell-faced beings
dancing in the center of a flaming lotus
billowing colorations from orange to red

Lattice of light,
tendrils of flesh, sweating moons, flayed skins of smoking
iguanas,
shriveled penises covered with tar,
rain of dead birds frozen in methane,
polished chunks of jade, devastated cables of twisted iron
sputtering arteries of burning oil

THE GIRLFRIEND

The girlfriend comes in nude running circles around the room depositing turkey feathers all around her. I have never seen her like this. Her beautiful auburn hair and fine Victorian features radiating a yellowish glow. But it is her persistent scratching that makes me do a double take. Having never seen her nude I am shocked to discover she has the body of a plucked hen. Her boyfriend told me she was different in the morning but I had no idea how different. Taking a lamb chop from the table she begins smearing a circle of lamb's blood in the middle of the kitchen floor and begins scrawling symbols and signs. I fear she will wreak havoc if I don't get her back to bed. "Now dear, you know it is best to have some tea at such an early hour." She looks at me in utter frustration the lamb chop in her mouth trying hard to complete the circle. "You've created quite a dilemma for me," I tell her. "Now what will I do for lunch?" She pays me no mind and continues scrawling signs around the circle. I leave her to her workings. She hasn't been the same since Enrique left her.

VEINED FLOWER

The disaster that greets us between
The sky & the sea
Is a face in flames
Wanting out of the world's torpor
Boarding a flight machine
We take off like gods
Able & fucking with new flesh
Fairies rot inside a soggy patch of bog
Bulbous & awkward
My hands reach down toward
Infernal regions
Here at the bathroom sink washing your sperm
Out of my hair
I am not born yet
Hold me

ZOMBIE

With a pinch of arsenic
the green cadaver comes back to life
his powdered heart fluttering a hummingbird
inside a quilted rose
pattern
sewing his eyelids shut
Rotten manna appears like curdled cheese on his foreskin
Elliptical monster
in a lens
Had I known you before holocaust
(entrails of worms)
my slumber would have been better spent on a
bed of nails
Beast Star People of the fourth chakra
nail my heart to the wall!

WHITE SMOKE

Frozen bats stick to the window
The rickety chair in the attic
sails out to sea
Pelican Woman
in a black boat
We cross the ancestral waters
of time

Osirus on a balcony of smoke
now you are in the fata morgana
lost among the ruins of
Tikal
dead flowers,
withered tree,
breath of ka-bird
dissolved in a husk
perfect sentence
hidden with meaning
my precious heart in a peacock's throat
palpitating beneath
a wounded galaxy

EAGLE BENEATH THE SEA

Trapped in the crosswalk of
fire-torn billboards
I see faces in the ruptured asphalt,
deer dancers on the tarmac
Dinosaurs unravel intestinal tracks of
Mojave sand pits
Mystic 8 on the freeway
Homer above the ruins
Grandeur of nothing, extravagance of emptiness
like elk horns covered with dandelions
picked clean as the vertebrae of
desert rocks crawling with ants
We are skeletons born from nothing
Our destiny is to follow
the eagle beneath the sea

CRACKED MIRROR

Exaggerated facial remarks of an actor in a Chinese opera
Cascading gowns of orange silk
Sheen of glass in a dragon's paw
You look for me
dancing nude in a painting by Hieronymus Bosch
wearing a crown of crabapples
scratching hex marks in the air

Enigma of silver globules eating at the chateau windows
The man in the suit having disappeared
into an oxygen tank
took the aeroplane home
to mama

Tree in a gaping mouth
hands on a mountain
I survey the landscape of your arms & belly
circumference of flesh
your hair still wet from exhaustion
your feet stitched tight
to the lips of whomever you just
loved

Green pigeons in the sequined night flowers
you look for me
five eyes inside a cracked mirror

CASA DEMENTIA

The house feverish
like an old syphilitic
water blisters appear above the flesh
of the plaster
cracking veins
across the walls

Coming up the stairway
the house tilts awkwardly
somewhere towards
the center of itself
Makes me laugh
at this crumpled house's encumbrances
its delirium, its ugly destitution
so close to my own
this house I live in

ELECTRIC FAN HAIKU

walking around
I am inspired to take
a trip
to the dump

•

clacking on its stand
the electric fan fills the room
with court *bugaku* music

•

clink of bottles, rustle of torn cardboard
trash for some
money for others

•

lyricism of rusty mattress springs
& torn lace curtains
that's all I know

•

stems, twigs,
sticky green crystals
sifting the leaf
she's stoned

•

am I bliss, am I opal
am I forgotten photo
hanging in your mind?

•

thin bones & turquoise
starlight & reeds
I am what I am

THE AEON

stirs in us
daemon/ brother/ Castor/ Pollux
moving from universe to galaxy to Netherworld
you are rose as I am serpent
wrapped around The Tree

Nude deities of the New Capricorn
I think of you on Menachim Elohim Street
blocked pathways to the L train
There is much work to be done on Malkuth
ramparts & bridges, turrets & towers
of the walled-in City of Lost Ladies
Do you dream of lost ladies as I dream of you
at the window?
Is it pills, alcohol & cigarettes,
    gunpowder and opium,
that ravish your already dead body?
To banish demons of the past
    old age & death
what new light must surround us?

Corrosive morning red clouds in the west Amenti's haze above
    the Parthenon
Ra born of Amun's bosom
reed boats to whirlpools of galactic blackness
egret on the salt marsh the look of
eternity just within reach

Long black fingers of silt,
you are pearl in the lotus,
as I am gold threads in brocade,

splintered cabinets of vermilion, broken caskets of myrrh,
you are seed & flame
as I am dust & mortar crumbling mud brick obelisk in the sun

VELVET CLAW

Web-fingered
with two brains of gelatin
& molasses
I touch you
like a tongue of flame
on the forehead of a catatonic saint

Hungry for the sticky parts
of your rotting soul
Do you know the sacred vow
to initiate orgies,
raise the dead, open vaults to the little bat-child
who brings damnation?
Do you know
a strange star protects us?

MILLENNIAL MISSIVE

Asoka, the iron wheel of this world teeters on its axis
as a golden age cries out to be born
an age of wisdom, generosity, loving kindness and compassion
not this catastrophe to lay low all illusion

Hungry ghosts grip at the wheel unable to feast at the tables
    laden with human corpses
Fields of vitreous sand this was once a desert an oil-rigged game
    of chance *no one wins*
Adolf Hitler appears at the summit meeting to sign the pact for
    the Novus Ordo Seclorum
The President's banker files the affidavit
Charles Chaplin and E.T. at The Sea of Tranquility landing

out of the vaults of burning money let fly upheaval accursed race
fossil fuel injectors in the suction engines running on marrow

Mother Durga rides her tiger
A group of children
holding hands
follow her
unwittingly
into the furnace of war

Annihilation
Apocalypse
These are the words written in cretinous scriptures
Massacre of the ten thousand fuchsia petals
Jealous gods are crashing their cymbals
It's Harry Crosby time in the West banking on junk bonds
    soaking in petro

the salt pits fortified with biologic hazard
so sleek, so stylish
the high-tech response to auto-destruction

A window
overlooking membranous stratosphere, how serpentine gleams
    matter devouring
its tail, blank auras sweeping away the feathers of being
That was my friend lost in that web-woven helix of plasma
Pain of a wilted flower
A hair trigger in the iron rain of black ash
Grandeur of iniquity
who writes the haunts of decimated sandalwood forests
Disposable world we inhabit, a jewel-encrusted mandala
set upon a seething ocean of misery

Written on the eve of the Persian Gulf War
January 1991

INVISIBLE WORLD
Song for the ancestors

See this hair?
You can have this hair
Long, black, Indian hair
All those dead Indians
will come back
to live inside you
Here! take this hair
and may it give you enough strength
to live a million lives

See these hands?
You can have these hands
You'll be surprised
at the things
they can do for you
Here! take these hands
and may you find enough love
to hold onto

See these eyes?
You can have these eyes
They can see very far
Here! take these eyes
and may you see
to the end of many skies

www.ingramcontent.com/pod-product-compliance
Lightning Source LLC
LaVergne TN
LVHW041300080426
835510LV00009B/810
* 9 7 8 0 6 1 5 5 3 5 5 8 6 *